21 COMMON MISTAKES OF YOUNG AND ADULT SINGLE LADIES

JONAH IDOKO

21 COMMON MISTAKES OF YOUNG AND ADULT SINGLE LADIES

Copyright © February 2024 by JONAH IDOKO

ISBN: 978-1-916650-28-2

Published by:
Mind2Global Oasis
mind2globaloasis@gmail.com

DISCLAIMER

This write-up does not result from psychological reasoning or moral intuitions, but the Holy Spirit inspires every part of this book. All personal experiences and stories shared are real life and truthful events and not fiction. It is purely a Christian book with biblical references. All biblical quotations are taken from the King James Version® copyright© 1982, Thomas Nelson, Inc., Publishers.

Contents

DEDICATION

This book is dedicated to the Trinity God: God the Father, Son, and Holy Spirit for the fountain of inspiration and provisions for this work.

ACKNOWLEDGEMENT

I return all the glory to God almighty for inspiration, wisdom, and direction for this book from start to finish.

Thank you so much, Dr. Mrs. Omotayo Fadoyebo, for your immense contribution to this book. You took time out of your tight schedule to review and authenticate this book from a moral and biological perspective.

I appreciate my enviable and energetic Pastor Cyril Jarumai (Area Pastor\Provincial Prayer Coordinator LP 67). Your impact on this book is tremendous and immeasurable. Thank you so much.

I appreciate my wonderful friends, Isah Josiah Joseph and Awoyode John Sunday. You were the first people I sent this write-up to, and you encouraged and pushed me.

Thank you so much, Mrs. Efe Ovhori, for your tremendous support of this great work.

I am so grateful to my dearly beloved brother Idoko Monday and my immediate family for your love and support.

Finally, to my dearly beloved wife, Mercy, thank you for being a great support throughout this project from start to finish. I love you so much.

FOREWORD

It was truly enlightening and instructive to read the manuscript written by Jonah Idoko, entitled "21 Common Mistakes of Young and Adult Single Ladies". In this book you will find more than just words on paper; you'll discover a guiding light, a beacon of hope, and a roadmap to reclaiming the power and purpose within you.

We live in a world that often seeks to erode our divine identity in order to diminish our worth, cloud our vision, and lead us astray from the path of true fulfillment. But here's the secret they don't want you to know: You have been created with unique qualities which are God-like; You are fearfully and wonderfully made. Yes, you, with all your quirks, flaws, and imperfections. You are a masterpiece sculpted by the hands of a loving Creator, imbued with infinite potential and boundless grace.

Throughout these pages, you'll be reminded of your kingdom identity, inherent worth, encouraged to embrace your uniqueness, and empowered to rise above the shadows of doubt and insecurity. Whether you're wrestling with self-doubt, low esteem or grappling with societal pressures, know that you are not alone. The author has penned these words to guide you through the valleys of uncertainty and ascend to the mountaintops of self-discovery and empowerment.

As you read, I urge you to approach each chapter with an open heart and a willingness to prayerfully confront the truths that may unsettle you. For it is in the depth of self-reflection that we find the seeds of growth and the courage to rewrite our stories.

Thanks, Jonah Idoko, for pouring your heart into your writing which is firmly rooted in scripture. I have no doubt that the spirit in the written word will speak to us today as we believe God for unending transformation in life.

Cyril Jarumai
Senior Pastor
RCCG Calvary Assembly Ikoyi.

INTRODUCTION

G od created man and woman with unique and special abilities. To many, the latter has enjoyed the bulk of these blessings than the former. This is because women are unique from men by God's design. Women are powerful and very unique in the way God created them. Their ability to multi-task, pay attention to details, perform tedious tasks, carry a child in their womb for nine months, and raise the child to adulthood is amazing.

However, as young and adult ladies, you can make mistakes that can rob you of these abilities and keep you in regret for the rest of your lives. Those mistakes are avoidable, and some can be corrected early enough.

This book, *"21 Common Mistakes of Young and Adult Single Ladies,"* is a divine revelation to help ladies identify those mistakes, teach them how to avoid them, and make corrections where necessary.

It touches almost all aspects of a lady's life and what is needed to prepare them to locate and make the right choice in marriage, and also helps them for the rest of their lives. Therefore, I implore you to approach reading this book with an open mind and pray along as you read through the pages for the Holy Spirit to enlighten your understanding.

CHAPTER ONE

HAVING LOW SELF-ESTEEM

---

*A man who is not defeated from the inside
(mind) can never be defeated. But once you
accept defeat from the inside there is nothing
anybody can do to help you.*

The best gift a woman can give herself is liking herself the way she is. You don't expect people to like you better than you like yourself. The way God created you is lovely and unique; you are the image of God.

Psalms 139:14 I will praise thee; for I am fearfully and wonderfully made: marvelous are thy works; and my soul knoweth right well.

Nobody can love you more than you love yourself. Self-love is not selfishness or pride; it's the appreciation of your worth and value in gratitude to God. So stop spending so much time complaining about the things you cannot change and focus on the good things about you. Just love yourself that way! You spend so much time telling yourself your eyes are too big or that your skin is too dark, short, and slim, but obviously, you can't change those things, so learn to appreciate yourself the way God makes you.

Matthew 6:27 Which of you, by taking thought, can add one cubit unto his stature?

Worry doesn't change anything but instead makes it look worse. You can only start being a superwoman when you start being yourself. Not everyone in the world would like you, no matter what, but some people will like you just the way you are. You can only know your true friends by being who you are. So, stop killing yourself and pretending to be another person for someone to like you. Every woman is beautiful and has her price, including you. Whichever way, there is a man out there yearning for you.

Whenever I sit with my male friends and discuss our choices for women, I discover that we all have different things we like in women. Some of my friends prefer slim ladies. They look portable and fitted, while others like chubby ladies because they're more glaring and command more respect. Others like their woman short, while some like them tall for different reasons. Sometimes, I will laugh profoundly as my friends mention some ridiculously incredible features they admire in a woman and eagerly look out for. But the truth is, nobody can make them change what they like because we are all created differently.

Don't keep yourself low, thinking nobody likes you. That particular reason you downgrade yourself might be why somebody else wants you. Start liking yourself, and you will see that everything about you will change completely. A man not defeated from the inside (mind) can never be defeated. But once you accept defeat from the inside, there is nothing anybody can do to help you.

You may be physically challenged or a victim of any natural circumstance, but you have got to love yourself and see yourself the way God sees you. There is no situation limiting anyone except the mind.

The truth is every man or woman has a reason to be weighed down by looks or life circumstances, but only those who have overcome those weights can reach their greatest potential. Be bold, be confident, be proud of yourself, build your self-esteem, and start seeing yourself differently, and your life will turn around drastically in no time.

Numbers 13:31-33 But the men that went up with him said, We be not able to go up against the people; for they are stronger than we.

And they brought up an evil report of the land which they had searched unto the children of Israel, saying, The land, through which we have gone to search it, is a land that eateth up the inhabitants thereof; and all the people that we saw in it are men of great stature.

And there we saw the giants, the sons of
Anak, which come of the giants: and we
were in our own sight as grasshoppers, and
so we were in their sight.

Don't be like some of the children of Israel who went
to spy on the land of Canaan and saw themselves as
grasshoppers before them. Because they saw
themselves as grasshoppers, that is how the children of
Anak saw them, too. Be bold and confident because
you are a child of the highest God. Declare the word of
God constantly upon your life. You can do all things
through Christ that strengthens you. Your glory and
beauty are not in your outward looks nor what you
have or don't have. The day you break free from low
self-image, you will realize that the things you feared
most are more afraid of you.

CHAPTER TWO

LIVING WITH A MAN WHO IS NOT YOUR HUSBAND

Cohabiting brings about "see finish" – This is a situation where someone gets too used to you and he becomes tired of you because you are cheaply available. When there is no price tag on an item there will be no value for it.

C ohabiting is very common nowadays, especially among students in school and young people in the city. Some ladies cohabit to get financial assistance, social security, or other material needs. Some do that due to love or the man promised to marry them.

This is an act of total disrespect for oneself, your family, and God. You present yourself cheaply if you move into the apartment of a man who is not married to you officially. You also disrespect your family, especially your parents, as you deprive them of their parental authority over you. No woman can give herself out in marriage; only her parents and family have that right. What the man you cohabit with will first think of you is whether you have good home training, and he will always look down on your parents. Additionally, it is a total dishonor to God and His orders. God's ordination for marriage is that a man and a woman are to leave their parents and cleave together to become one flesh after the due process of marital rites.

> *Genesis 2:24: "Therefore shall a man leave his father and his mother, and shall cleave unto his wife: and they shall be one flesh."*

It doesn't matter how long you have been living with a man who is not legally married to you, whether you have a child or children together; it's called **Cohabiting**. If your bride price is not paid and the consent of both families is not given, then you are not married, and if you are not married to any man, it is not approved by God because no physical and spiritual evidence legalized that union. Every sexual act you have together in that state is a sin against God.

While I was on campus as an undergraduate, I knew many guys and girls living together in school as husband and wife, but they portrayed themselves as "singles" in the church and any time they returned home for holidays. Before we graduated, some had issues with each other and parted, while some went their separate ways soon after we left school.

Cohabiting brings about *"see finish"* – This is a situation where someone gets too used to you and becomes tired of you because you are cheaply available. There will be no value for an item with no price tag.

You will not be treasured if you present yourself as a cheap item. Jewelry that you travel from Nigeria to Dubai to buy at a costly price will be more treasured than the one that came to you on your street by the hand of the hawkers.

Some ladies who get themselves involved in cohabiting may get pregnant, and because you don't want people to know you got pregnant outside wedlock, you start taking drugs and things that can become a threat to your life and future conception.

Whatever benefits you enjoy from a man by living with him without the benefit of marriage is not comparable to the disadvantage. Stop drawing attention to yourself and creating negative impressions that you already have a man in your life; when that man puts you away, you may have chased away serious suitors.

From my experience, women living with men with whom they are not legally married are most likely prone to domestic abuse. On campus those days, I remember counseling some ladies who were victims of such abuse where the guy woke up at night and started demanding for husband and wife's intimacy, whereas the lady had to read for exams that she had the next day.

Luke 15:17-18 And when he came to himself, he said, How many hired servants of my father's have bread enough and to spare, and I perish with hunger!

I will arise and go to my father and will say unto him, Father, I have sinned against heaven, and before thee, "

Ladies, please return to your senses as the prodigal son did, pack your luggage, and leave. The right time to do it is now! If he is not ready to marry, why not let him wait till he is ready and let him look for you then. Don't waste your precious years living with someone who is not your husband; who knows if the right man is looking for you now, but you are nowhere to be found because you are where you are not supposed to be? God will always make way for you when you return to him genuinely and get yourself together.

CHAPTER THREE

NOT BEING RESPECTFUL

Some ladies experience delay in their marriages due to the fact that they are too proud and have a different opinion of what marriage should be. Others get married but experience marital crisis because they find it difficult to respect their spouse.

A s a young lady, you need to lower your ego. Lowering your ego does not mean you should go below the acceptable standard of God for your life. Instead, it means that you should know that taking too highly of yourself is a sure way to come down.

Ephesians 5:22-23 "Wives, submit
yourselves unto your own husbands, as
unto the Lord. For the husband is the head
of the wife, even as Christ is the head of the
church: and he is the savior of the body."

No man can stand a disrespectful and nagging woman. Naturally, every man sees himself as a king and likes to be treated that way, but when you treat men the other way, there will be problems.

Humility is a powerful virtue that can make a woman attractive to any man. Women are wonderfully made with peculiar and great features; however, they can attain their greatest potential when they submit to a man. God didn't give headship to the woman (Eve) but to the man (Adam). This doesn't mean that women are less important, but it is a matter of responsibility given by God, and we cannot change it. Society these days clamors for gender equality, where the rights, duties, and opportunities of individuals will not depend on whether they are male or female. This could be viewed in the larger society as a good thing; however, no matter your achievement as a woman, you must submit, stay humble, and allow God to be the builder of your home.

Some ladies experience delays in their marriages because they are too proud and have a different opinion of what marriage should be. Others get married but experience marital crises because they find it difficult to respect their spouse.

The word *"submit"* means to *bring under subjection.* You may be well to do as a lady, but you have to submit. You may be well-learned or eloquent in speech and understanding, but it is your duty as a wise woman to be submissive. The issue of humility can't be window-dressed or underestimated. It's either you are humble, or you are not.

I know a lady in my town who is now advanced in age but has yet to marry because stories have it that she always neglected and downgraded any man that came her way. In the olden days, people married brides from the community and took them to their sons in the city, even without courtship or the sons ever meeting the brides. One of the significant criteria they use in making those choices of wives for their children is the level of purity, respect, and dignity the ladies are known to have within the community and towards God.

God didn't tell the woman to love the man because He knows that the nature of women is love. Women are soft-hearted, so they will not have issues loving a man, but the question is "if they will submit." The way a man knows a woman loves him is the level of her submission. Most women who come for counseling will be crying with tears, telling how much they love their husbands, but each time we try to investigate further, we will find out that the problem is not love but submission at home.

If you don't practice submission as a single lady, you cannot do it in marriage. There is an adage among the *Idoma*-speaking people of BENUE, NIGERIA, that says, *"Stooping low doesn't make someone short."* Humility doesn't take anything from you but instead adds to you. People will value you more by discovering your worth than you show them or telling them at any given opportunity you have.

16

The real beauty of a woman is seen in her character. You must make it a deliberate practice to stay humble to everyone, small or great, no matter your beauty or possessions as a woman.

I know some men who are not worth much as husbands but receive great favors because their wives have unbeatable excellent characteristics of humility.

1 Samuel 25:3, 23-24

"Now the name of the man was Nabal, and the name of his wife Abigail: and she was a woman of good understanding, and of a beautiful countenance: but the man was churlish and evil in his doings, and he was of the house of Caleb.

And when Abigail saw David, she hasted, and lighted off the ass, and fell before David on her face, and bowed herself to the ground,

And fell at his feet, and said, Upon me, my lord, upon me let this iniquity be: and let thine handmaid, I pray thee, speak in thine

The story of David, Abigail, and Nabal in 1 Samuel 25 is a good example of a woman who saved her household because of her humility and outstanding character lifestyle. Nabal, Abigail's husband, was a proud and foolish man, but Abigail was wise and humble. She quickly made an arrangement to meet up with David before disaster happened to her household. Note that Abigail also alighted from the ass when she met David. Alighting from the ass is a show of humility and submissiveness. Some ladies, even if they see a potential suitor they, still sit on the ass high and unbending, and they miss their opportunities. It is high time you stopped being proud so that God can promote you.

James 4:10: “Humble yourselves in the
sight of the Lord, and he shall lift you up. ”

18

CHAPTER FOUR

NOT BEING ABLE TO MANAGE AVAILABLE RESOURCES

In life there is no measure of exactly how much resources will be enough and how much will not be enough; it all depends on who is managing it.

B efore I met my wife, the beautiful lady Mercy, I was already looking out and trusting God for her to be a good manager of money and materials. This is because I would have finished spending or giving out my last card before realizing it. Thank God that when my wife came, she was the perfect complement for that area of my life, and I decided to make her our treasurer. Not only where cash is concerned but also for household items and consumables. I am more extravagant than she is. She keeps a good record of consumables and when they need to be replenished. Meanwhile, I am the opposite; I notice when we have already run out and need to restock. I usually tend to buy those things I didn't budget for, but the case is not the same with my wife.

Most men tend to be more extravagant than women. I know most men like me will appreciate a woman who is a good manager of resources.

Proverbs 31:15-16

"She riseth also while it is yet night and giveth meat to her household and a portion to her maidens.

She considereth a field, and buyeth it: with the fruit of her hands she planteth a vineyard."

The story of the Virtuous woman in Proverbs 31 shows how she manages her home and cares for her husband

and children. She may not necessarily be the primary source of the home's finances, but she knows how to channel any available resources in the areas of need at home.

If you are a lady and extravagant, you are about to experience a disaster in marriage. You must learn how to manage money as a lady. No matter the amount you have or are being given, it can never be enough if not well managed. Learn how to start working with budgets because the sole responsibility of home management is on you as a woman. Most men are not as meticulous in managing the home properly as women will do, but it takes a woman with sound financial discipline to do so.

You may not know the kind of husband that God will give you, either wealthy or still trying to build his life, so you must avoid being wasteful by all means. If you marry an already established rich man, then good for you, but then he might not give you the whole world every day, but you must learn how to make do with what you have. Also, if you marry a man still growing financially, you may not have it in abundance, but you have to devise a means of working your budget to match the available resources while you trust God for rainy days.

In life, there is no measure of how many resources will be enough and how many will not; it all depends on who manages it—for instance, two families each comprised a husband, wife, and child. One may have a ₦200,000 budget for feeding the family for the whole month, and the other family may have a budget of ₦50,000 to feed the family for the entire month. If care is not taken, the woman managing #200,000 for a month's feeding allowance may complain that it is insufficient. In contrast, the woman who manages #50,000 for a month's feeding allowance may not have any complaints as she manages the few resources well. Everybody likes enjoyment and will probably want a buffet every day, but you must know your level and stage in life and adjust your budget to match it.

At times when I may have finished all the money I have on me, and my wife realizes, she brings out some little reimbursement when I least expect. This money she will bring will be her reserve from the little allowance I gave her for monthly home upkeep. Wise women always have some reserve, no matter how little, because that little will go a long way at critical times. There is no home that doesn't experience critical times at one point or another, no matter how wealthy. If your husband is a businessman, there may be downtimes, negatively affecting cash flow and the family's budget. Also, if your spouse is an employee, salaries may sometimes not come as expected, or he may be disengaged from work. If you are not a good manager in those times of crisis, it may result in your home experiencing financial and material shortfalls. As a woman, you must know how to adjust and acclimatize to financial conditions.

Don't wait until you are married; start now! You don't need to buy expensive hair attachments\wigs or clothes constantly. If there is no money to buy chicken, then buy beef. If you can't afford beef, buy fish or *ponmo (Nigerian name for skin)*. You must be a master when it comes to adaptation as a woman. There are days you may not even be able to afford protein, but you must still learn how to improvise and eat cheerfully, knowing that good days are coming soon.

Incredible women always perform wonders with little things. A pot of soup cooked with #30,000 may not taste better than another pot of soup cooked with #10,000, depending on who cooked it and how the materials are managed. Master your personal life and how you manage your resources now, and you will be the superwoman every man dreams of having.

I once met a lady, and we talked for some time. One thing led to another, and she said she can't eat any food without meat (protein), even if it was *garri*. Otherwise, she would throw up. She said she must have plenty of meat on her table whenever she wants to eat. I knew my income then and could not afford that consistently in every condition, so I had to *take off*.

Many families are under pressure now because the woman wants the most expensive of everything, not necessarily because it is required but because the woman wants to measure up to other people. Don't allow anybody to influence your budget unless you all have the same income and ambitions.

CHAPTER FIVE

USING SEX TO KEEP A MAN

Men have more respect for a woman they love and they have not slept with than a woman they have already slept with. Don't think that sleeping with a man will make him stay with you and marry you as a lady.

Sex before marriage is a sin, and it can open up windows for lack of trust and other negative consequences in marriage.

1 Corinthians 6:18-20

"Flee fornication. Every sin a man doeth is without the body; but he that committeth fornication sinneth against his own body.

What, know ye not that your body is the temple of the Holy Ghost which is in you, which ye have of God, and ye are not your own?

For ye are bought with a price: therefore glorify God in your body, and in your spirit, which is God's."

The truth is that when a man sees the lady he really would like to marry, he will not so much be desperate about having sex with her. I have asked many men about this and have personal experience, too. So if any man is telling you he wants to have sex with you because he loves you or because the sex will make both of you closer, know that it is a lie.

Men have more respect for a woman they love, and they have not slept with than a woman they have already slept with. Don't think that sleeping with a man will make him stay with you and marry you as a lady. Ladies who make this mistake later end up in regret because the man may not stay. As a matter of fact, he soon gets tired and leaves. Man's sexual desires can never be satisfied unless in marriage and with the fear of God, so stop trying to fulfill the desire of any man so that he can stay with you as a single lady. You are not an *Aboki Suya* that men will taste before they buy. You will end up giving so much testing for free, and they will not buy.

Studies have shown that 90% of men who approach ladies are for sex and other selfish reasons and nothing more. If you quickly throw yourself on his bed, thinking you will give him sex to keep him, that means you are being foolish. The same man will go to another girl who is ready to give him to meet his sexual desires. You can't know, and you will not be able to get a sincere man if you are busy sleeping around.

Well, you may think that submitting to his immoral adventures will get him attracted to you and marry you; this may be a delusion that you may live to regret. No desperation should push you to do so because it will not end the way you think. Some ladies even go to the extent of getting pregnant for a guy intentionally, thinking she will tie him down because of the baby. This is why we have many Baby Mamas these days. If you observe, most baby daddies will have more than one Baby Mama because the first one couldn't keep him but has just exposed him and given him more reasons to go after other girls.

You don't have to build a family by forcing a guy to marry you because, in marriage, you will continue to force him to love and accept you. If you eventually have him, he may go after other women, and at that time, you will end up in bitterness.

Men tend to forget more quickly the ladies they have had sex with than the ones they love but didn't have sex with. Even though the one they have sex with flashes across their minds, it is just for the events, but there is no value attached to it in their minds other than the sexual exploits. If they have another chance with that same lady, the aim is to sleep with her again, and that is all. When a man sleeps with you as a lady, you have lost all your values in his sight, and if he still wants to keep you, maybe it is for future exploitation, but the fact is that you have depreciated in his mind.

Recently, a friend asked me to accompany him to his intended in-law's house. On our way, we started talking, and he told me how he met this lady on campus, and they started dating. All efforts he made to sleep with her were to no avail for many years on campus. The lady always insisted she wanted to keep herself for her future husband. I then told my friend that this lady must be very beautiful, and he said that she was the least physically attractive among all the girls he had ever dated, but her behavior made her outstanding. When we talked, they had left campus for over three years, and he couldn't forget about this lady because she refused to jump into bed with him. The only woman that could come to his mind as a wife material is that lady who stood by her decision. Any man who left you because you didn't allow him to have sex with you didn't love you in the first place. The one that loves you will stay with you because you didn't have sex together.

There are many things that a lady can regret after going to bed with a man, thinking she will keep him. One of them is that the lady can get pregnant outside wedlock. I have seen situations where some guys will deny being responsible for pregnancies and allow the girls to face the shame alone together with the responsibilities. If you are ready for marriage, all you need to do is pray and ask God to give you a husband of your own, a man you don't need to please with your body or try to force him to love.

CHAPTER SIX

USING ALL YOUTHFUL AGE TO PURSUE CAREER

Every woman has different prime times in life. This is usually the time when suitor will be flooding your ways, especially from age eighteen to thirty.

As a lady, it is good to establish yourself, have something to do, and not be a liability. I am not against ladies trying to be independent of their future spouses. It is good to be financially independent to help your future husband. But the truth is that that should not be done to the detriment of the future.

Every woman has different prime times in life. This is usually when suitors flood your way, especially from age eighteen to thirty. As you pursue careers and other personal goals, you must think of marriage or having a healthy relationship that can lead to marriage as you pursue your pursuit. The life of a woman is like a flower. Flowers have times when they blossom and look attractive, usually early in the morning. When you see a flower rise early in the morning, you will desire to have it, but at noon or by evening, after the sun has scorched it, it will look dull and feeble.

Ecclesiastes 3:1-2

"To everything, there is a season and a time to every purpose under the heaven:

A time to be born, and a time to die; a time to plant, and a time to pluck up that which is planted."

God has put time into everything, and so is the case of a woman. There are best times to marry or start thinking of marriage because of several factors. There is nothing wrong with having a genuine relationship while you pursue academics or careers. I married my wife in her 300 level at the University, and we both agreed that she would finish her studies regardless of the marriage. If you meet the right person who believes in your dreams and is ready to support you, why not?

Many ladies believe they will pursue careers until thirty to thirty-five years before they give attention to any man. They think that any time they are ready for marriage, men will flood them like they did at a young age. Men may come, but so many will come for what you have achieved, not love. Getting someone you can build together is better than waiting to be made yourself first.

Deuteronomy 32:30

"How should one chase a thousand, and two put ten thousand to flight, except their Rock had sold them, and the LORD had shut them up?"

The efforts of two people put together are always better than one. The Bible says *if one person can chase a thousand, two will be able to chase ten thousand.* This biblical mathematics is a mystery, but it is very real. Logical mathematics will say if one person will chase a thousand, then two will chase a thousand times two, which is two thousand. Still, the design and principle of God's synergy is that two minds that agree on a particular purpose will have the strength of ten men.

Many who made this mistake are running from one prayer mountain to another. Some of these ladies were not victims because they were pursuing careers. Still, because they were busy rejecting and selecting suitors, they rejected him even when the right person came their way, thinking other men would continue to come. So, while trying to get stable financially and have a stellar career, you must remember that late marriages come with some pertinent issues.

Firstly, if you take too long before marriage, there might be difficulty with conception and fertility. Research has shown that fertility decreases with age, and the ability to have healthy children also decreases. This is because children born to older parents have a considerable risk of Down's Syndrome and other complications. This risk is more pronounced in women than men. There is reduced quality and quantity of egg production in women with age, leading to more difficulty in conception and an increased risk of miscarriage. Women naturally enter into their menopause in their 40s and 50s. This will partially or entirely bring to an end their menstrual cycles, hence making it difficult or impossible to conceive.

Secondly, there might be an increase in the risk of health issues like fibroid in women who experience late marriage. According to studies by The Chief Consultant Radiotherapist and Oncologist of the National Hospital, Abuja, Dr Abdurasaq Oyesegun (Vanguard Newspaper September 4, 2012), he advised women to *marry in their 20s to avoid the possibility of developing fibroid.* Oyesegun said *the uterus is designed to carry babies, and when the uterus cannot carry babies, then the muscles of the uterus increase and result in fibroids.*

A friend to a female friend of mine developed fibroids as a result of age and because she was still single. First, she was operated upon, and after some time, the fibroid grew back again. She was operated on the second time. After the second operation, she didn't wait to retake the chance because the doctor told her the growth might come back again; she quickly got pregnant for a guy who she didn't love because of the fear of the fibroids growing back and preventing conception. She didn't even plan to have a family with this guy. I am not saying her decision to get pregnant is right, but she could have averted all that pressure and wrong decision if she was married before now. I was curious and asked my friend why her girlfriend had not been married before now, and she told me that her friend had been selective right from time, even though many suitors had come her way. Please don't let your case be like this lady who went through all these problems yet made a wrong decision that doesn't glorify God.

Thirdly, some ladies who marry late or marry when they are already made find it challenging to adjust to situations in marriage as they are too used to their ways. It is easier to adjust to another person's needs or likings when you are younger. Since you have already been set in your ways for a long time, you prioritize your freedom over building a family. This might lead to some ladies finding it uninteresting to go the family way, having been used to single life and freedom over the years.

Also, the future family that you want to have it all made for before marriage may come at a time when you don't have the strength and capacity to be up and doing for them when they need you most due to old age. God is a God of timing, and he has set nature in the order in which they are, and it will only take his grace and mercy to change the order of things. You never can tell if He will do it in your case, so you need to use wisdom to avoid regret.

CHAPTER SEVEN

LOOKING FOR A MAN WHO HAS IT ALL

It's a good thing if God blesses you with a man who is well to do and has it already made, but the truth is that not every woman's destiny is designed to start with five steps upward the ladder. The beginning doesn't really matter, what is important is where you are headed.

"The LORD killeth, and maketh alive: he bringeth down to the grave, and bringeth up.

The LORD maketh poor, and maketh rich: he bringeth low, and lifteth up.

He raiseth up the poor out of the dust, and
lifteth up the beggar from the dunghill, to
set them among princes, and to make them
inherit the throne of glory: for the pillars of
the earth are the LORD'S, and he hath set
the world upon them." – 1 Samuel 2:6-8

I have seen very wretched and poor people lifted by God. I have also seen people who are rich in millions of dollars become extremely poor. God uses these scenarios to teach us lessons that the life and achievement of every man are in his hands. From my research, nobody can be the world's richest man for over ten years. This shows that wealth comes and goes. The power to be at the top is not in any man's hand but God's. You can't write off anyone because God can bless and lift anyone; it doesn't take God anything to raise the poor out of the dust, lift the beggar from the dunghill, and set them among princes.

Zechariah 4:10 For who hath despised the
day of small things? For they shall rejoice
and shall see the plummet in the hand of
Zerubbabel with those seven; they are the

eyes of the LORD, which run to and fro
through the whole earth.

One constant thing that happens to man in life is change. Some of my classmates who were always behind in class and not very popular are now in better positions than those who bragged in class in those days. This is attributed to self-development and living a purpose-driven life.

It's good if God blesses you with a man who is well-to-do and has it already made, but the truth is that not every woman's destiny is designed to start with five steps up the ladder. The beginning doesn't matter; what is important is where you are headed. I have seen that most great people who shake the world didn't start great but grew gradually. Nobody climbs the ladder from the top to bottom but rather from the bottom, taking one step at a time until they reach the top. If you set the criteria that the man you will marry must have it all, then you are making a great mistake.

The person working in the highest-paying organization today may lose his job tomorrow, or the organization may shut down. Businesses may blossom today and become dull tomorrow; even if the capital is in billions of dollars, it can vanish quickly with just one business crisis. You cannot use today's achievement of someone to judge who you marry unless you are a gold digger looking for where to hit and run.

Unfortunately, marriage is not a sprint but a marathon. Suppose you marry or choose your relationship based on material possessions or bank account statements. In that case, you will not be able to stay in that marriage tomorrow if the situation turns negative. But the reality is that things change, and life is not always rosy.

Proverbs 23:5 "Wilt thou set thine eyes upon that which is not, for riches certainly make themselves wings; they fly away as an eagle toward heaven."

Think about having a wealthy partner, but think more of a righteous and God-fearing man because you can be rich and not enjoy it. You can have all you want, but if you are married to an abusive man, then you will live in sorrow for the rest of the marriage.

Proverbs 11:4 "Riches profit not in the day of wrath: but righteousness delivereth from death."

Surprisingly, some ladies don't care to know the source of the wealth, but they go for it once the man has cars and can gift them flashy things. Many strange things happen these days; ladies must be cautious about how some pursue material things; otherwise, they may end up in the wrong hands. Any man who doesn't have the fear of God has no cover over his possessions. It can vanish once the devil strikes.

When a man walks up to you, let not the size of his pocket or possessions be the first thing you will check. Check first if the man is a born-again child of God and truly fears God. You can never underrate what a man who fears God can become.

Proverbs 22:29 Seest thou a man diligent in his business? He shall stand before kings; he shall not stand before mean men.

Another thing you should look out for in a man is if he has anything to do and is diligent with what he is doing.

Those two criteria, "work and diligence," are what the Bible says will make a man stand before kings and not mere men. I am not saying you should marry any man with nothing to do, but at least he must have something to do with his hand. Either a job, a trade, a business, or a skill that is legal and verifiable. He must not necessarily be well established in what he is doing, but once he is diligent, that is all he needs to stand before kings later in life. The word "*diligence* " means consistency and persistence. Someone serious and not lazy, determined, and striving to become somebody in life is who you should look out for to marry.

There is power in two like-minded people building up together in a relationship. When you trust a man and build up with him, he will value you more because he always remembers you are part of his story. You were there to encourage him and give him the support to carry on.

The already made you are looking for might not come forever; even if he comes, he might not be the right man for you, so why not go for the one who is not made yet but has the potential to build and become what you want tomorrow? Stop wasting your time looking for a wealthy man by all means.

CHAPTER EIGHT

SEX FOR MONEY

There is no prostitute that doesn't have an excuse or reasons to give as to why she indulge in the acts. But there is no excuse that is genuine enough to warrant you selling your body for any price.

S ome ladies are fully or partially into the business of sleeping around with men for the sake of getting money or other benefits in return. It is called *prostitution* – Anything you do with your private parts to bring you money or favor by any means is whoredom. Unfortunately, our society today has many sweet names for it, thereby making it look trivial. Some call it hookups, hustle, runs, business, etc. But whatever name you call it, it's condemnable.

Ephesians 5:5 For this ye know, that no whoremonger, nor unclean person, nor covetous man, who is an idolater, hath any inheritance in the kingdom of Christ and God.

The scripture above shows that anybody involved in the act of whoredom (prostitution) has no inheritance with God. Prostitution is abominable before God. Some ladies are entirely into the act, where they hire a house, and different men come in to sleep with them in exchange for money. Some ladies do it part-time, while others do it based on pressure and needs they want to meet. Some ladies in the comfort of their rooms negotiate the price of their bodies before going out to meet their clients. Whichever way, it is an act of prostitution.

Some ladies specialize in *sugar daddies.* That is to say, their preference is for older married men. They are aware of this, yet they have affairs with the man for whatever personal benefits and cause trouble in families. An ancient paradigm says, "Any water you know you will not like to drink, it is better not to be used to wash your face because it will enter your mouth in the process." What you don't want to have others do to you, don't do to others as well because what goes around usually comes around in life.

No prostitute doesn't have an excuse or reasons to give as to why she indulges in the acts. But there is no excuse that is genuine enough to warrant you selling your body for any price. Some may hang the blame on unemployment; others may say because they lost their parents or because a crisis in their family pushed them to it. Meanwhile, others will say because they are in school and can't meet the demands or because the critical conditions of their parents and loved ones and a desire to help out forced them into that lifestyle.

There is no situation you find yourself in today that somebody else has not faced before and stayed strong without ending up in prostitution. Situations don't make men, but decisions do. Whatever situation you find yourself in, it is not that situation that tells who you are at the end of the day, but it is the quality of your decision.

Hebrews 12:1 Wherefore seeing we also are compassed about with so great a cloud of witnesses, let us lay aside every weight, and the sin which doth so easily beset us, and let us run with patience the race that is set before us.

Some witnesses have passed through more difficult challenges and came out through those challenges, not by selling their bodies. You don't have any excuse; it is just your choice to do it.

Matthew 16:26 For what is a man profited, if he shall gain the whole world, and lose his own soul? Or what shall a man give in exchange for his soul?

Any money or favor you receive to give out your body is like selling out your soul in exchange. No amount of money or service is worth the value of your soul. Jesus Christ said even the whole world will not profit a man to lose his soul. Your body is too valuable to be paid for with money or favors in exchange. Any man who offers you money or service and is demanding for your body, please decline it without thinking twice because the offer cannot be compared to the value of your soul.

Sex is not just entering your body and coming out; it is far beyond that. Sex involves a lot of exchange and receiving, both physically and spiritually. Each time you have sex, something happens to your body and your soul. Spirits are exchanged into your soul, and you exchange your spirit and virtues in return. Although you may feel normal after the whole thing, it is far beyond that.

Hosea 4:10

For they shall eat, and not have enough: they shall commit whoredom, and shall not increase: because they have left off to take heed to the LORD.

From the passage above, it shows clearly that there is no tangible benefit to prostitution. I have interviewed some girls who are into prostitution, and one of the questions I usually ask them is, "When are you going to stop?". Their usual answer is to gather more money to do one or two things before they stop. Some have been in it for years, saying they need more time to gather enough money to quit. It will never be enough; they can't get what they want forever because any money earned through that means is accursed. If you do runs or hookups to get money, you can only spend it on things that will make you get more runs or more hookups because the source is not genuine.

Ezekiel 23:3

And they committed whoredoms in Egypt;
they committed whoredoms in their youth:
there were their breasts pressed, and there
they bruised the teats of their virginity.

Apart from not being able to get anything substantial from selling your body, you stand the chance of contracting sexually transmitted diseases and infections like HIV, Syphilis, Gonorrhea, Hepatitis, etc. You also may be at the risk of losing your physical body structure. The Bible is particular about losing your breast structure and your virginity or sexual organ orientation by continuing in the act of whoredom. This may cause hitches between some husbands and wives in marriage because the woman's body is wholly disoriented as a result of the woman's habits previously.

Hosea 2:4

And I will not have mercy upon her children; for they are the children of whoredoms.

Also, the Bible mentions that anybody who involve in whoredom and their children will not receive the mercy of God. This shows that prostitution is a curse upon their unborn children. Some of the women who involved themselves in prostitution and their children also end up in the same evil lifestyle because it has become a curse on them.

Revelation 21:8

But the fearful, and unbelieving, and the abominable, and murderers, and whoremongers, and sorcerers, and idolaters, and all liars, shall have their part in the lake which burneth with fire and brimstone: which is the second death.

Finally, the last judgment for those who indulge in whoredom is the lake of fire, which burns with fire and brimstone. You don't want to end up in hell at the end of your journey on earth, so make up your mind not to sell your soul in exchange for the little need you have today. God has a way of coming through for all who are patient and wait for him in critical need. Don't be influenced by friends or anything to sell your body.

Don't waste your youthful years on these acts, thinking you have found a smart and easy way of making ends meet; you can be addicted to this lifestyle and never get out of it quickly. Instead, wait on God to send the right man your way so that you can settle down in your own house and stop throwing evil baggage into your future. An adage says, *"Where a child eats and stains his mouth with red oil, if not verified, he may come out with blood stain one day from that same place."* This means that as evil looks rosy instantly, if not curtailed, it may be deadly tomorrow.

CHAPTER NINE

NOT BEING CHEERFUL

---

*Staying cheerful as a lady has a way of
naturally drawing people to you. As a young
lady you are like a customer service agent.
You need to stay cheerful always and keep a
lively spirit; this is the only way to win
people and have good friends.*

Years ago, I was privileged to work in a
commercial bank as a sales agent. Before we
started working formally, we had to go
through onboarding and orientation, where we were
taught the ethics and cultures of the bank, as well as
the job description. We were first taught to smile and
be cheerful when attending to customers. During the
training, I asked, *"What if you are emotionally down*

or have some personal issues that are bothering you?." The facilitator responded that being cheerful is compulsory in all conditions notwithstanding. Once you enter the banking hall gate, you must drop all emotions and worries and put a big smile on your face. Customers don't understand your emotions and have no time to explain why you are not cheerful; all they know is that your cheerful face is inviting and evidence that you are happy to have them.

Anything less than being cheerful with customers is not acceptable as a customer service agent. The easiest way to get sacked from a commercial bank is to be rude and unhappy with customers. It is believed that losing a customer means losing four other potential customers. This is because the customer that you lost will tell at least four other people that your services are poor and discourage them from patronizing you.

There is nobody who doesn't like a happy and cheerful person, but nobody wants to be around a sad person.

Proverbs 17:22

"A merry heart doeth good like a medicine:
but a broken spirit drieth the bones."

A merry heart is like a medicine that heals. Everyone on earth wants healing for one reason or the other. I have never seen anybody who says he wants to be sorrowful or feels like being unhappy today, but people instead look for ways of making themselves happy and keeping their spirits up. This is why it is good to keep a cheerful attitude to attract people to yourself. The world is full of challenges and reasons for people to be depressed or weighed down, so everybody would instead go for an excited person, either as a friend or a partner in whatever way.

Staying cheerful as a lady has a way of naturally drawing people to you. As a young lady, you are like a customer service agent. You must always stay cheerful and lively; this is the only way to win people and have good friends. A sad-looking person is unapproachable; the look alone terrifies. Their looks make it easy to identify a lion or a tiger, which are intimidating and terrifying. You don't need a mature lion to roar before you get grabbed by fear, but just sighting it alone is enough for you to panic. If you are a lady, people will run miles from you and always wear a lion look.

We once had a receptionist in my former workplace; she was lively and cheerful whenever you saw her. Once she is seated at the front desk as you enter, she will give you this natural smile that makes you forget every stress in your mind. The next thing you will do is smile back at her. Everybody in the office, including her colleagues and customers, is very fond of her because of the joyful atmosphere she creates around herself.

I did my compulsory National Youth Service in a company in Lagos. During my service year, Tolu and I served in the same department as Corps members. He was the very cheerful and lively type. He was very active and fun to be with, making it easy for him to make friends with almost everybody, including senior managers. I loved him, as did everyone in the office, including our Head of Department and Manager. Over time, I saw my Head of Department and Manager's preference for him because of his unique attitude. Although I tried to learn from him and catch up, he had already built the first impression that made him irreplaceable in the hearts of everyone. Eventually, we rounded up the one-year compulsory Youth Service, and the company retained him and gave him an employment offer while I wasn't given the offer. I didn't need to ask why this happened because I already knew the obvious reason. This was not because he was more skilled and hard-working than me but because of his cheerful personality. He was often absent from work on flimsy excuses but was pardoned. The office would know he was not there each day because the atmosphere of happiness he created was second to none.

You can't keep a sad or unfriendly face as a lady and expect the right man to come your way. To live cheerfully should not be what you window dress or pretend about, but you must consciously make it a habit. When being cheerful, you don't need to be selective; let everyone around you feel it and receive the life-giving spirit that comes from you.

Proverbs 15:13 A merry heart maketh a cheerful countenance: but by sorrow of the heart the spirit is broken.

The nature of women should be characterized by softness. Usually, most men are harder in nature than women. When you keep a long face, you look like a man, and according to Coulumb's law of electricity, like charges repel while unlike charges attract each other. People often say you look more beautiful when you smile, but you tend to look more ugly when you frown. The beauty observed when you smile might not be due to the transfiguration of your face but the emotional effects that the smile you give creates in people's hearts and how you lift their spirits. Keeping a sad face makes you look uninviting and can even make you age quickly because it takes more facial muscles to frown than it takes to smile.

2 Corinthians 9:7

"Every man according as he purposeth in his heart, so let him give; not grudgingly, or of necessity: for God loveth a cheerful giver."

The scripture above clearly shows that giving to God must be done cheerfully because God loves a cheerful giver. It is not in the plan of God for you not to be cheerful going through your days. The same way God loves a cheerful giver is the way men love a cheerful individual. Always be noticeably happy and cheerful, no matter the challenge or what you see.

CHAPTER TEN

NOT BEING BORN AGAIN

There is something about being genuinely in Christ and in active service for God. This will make you discover yourself, bring out the best in you and guide you in the right direction in life.

There is something about being genuinely in Christ and active service for God. This will make you discover yourself, bring out the best in you, and guide you in the right direction in life. Everyone created by God is created with a purpose to fulfill a destiny specially designed by God. Only God has the blueprint and the original manuscript in his hands. You can only access this manuscript when you are genuinely connected with God. When you acknowledge God, it's easier to locate your purpose and go in the right direction.

If you are genuinely born again, most of these mistakes we discuss will be taken care of because God will always instruct and guide your paths and help you make the right decisions in life. People who have yet to surrender to God always make mistakes because they are the ones who direct their paths, not God. Surrendering your life to God is more of an advantage to you personally than it is to God. Some people think living a righteous life is like bondage, but it keeps you from the wrong steps and costly mistakes.

> *Daniel 11:32: "And such as do wickedly against the covenant shall he corrupt by flatteries: but the people that do know their God shall be strong, and do exploits."*

Doing exploits in life and making positive impacts is by knowing your God. No man or woman can attain their greatest potential unless connected to God.

Women have a lot to do in our world and society today, but those who will be able to do this are true to themselves and God. There are no limits to which women can go; if only they can stay connected to God to help them. Thank God for women like Esther and Deborah in their times. As we see in the Bible, these women were at the forefront, leading the course of God and doing exploits in their time because they were women who feared God. Throughout the scripture, there is no move of God where women are left out as they always perform a great part in everything God wants to do on earth. As a lady, you cannot affect your generation positively if you don't have a solid foundation in God.

> *Proverbs 31:30-31 Favour is deceitful, and beauty is vain: but a woman that feareth the LORD shall be praised.*
>
> *Give her of the fruit of her hands, and let her works praise her in the gates."*

No matter how beautiful you look as a lady or the favor you receive, you will not be much talked about if you don't fear God. Your beauty may attract men to you as a woman, but without the fear of God and good character, you cannot keep them. The real beauty of a woman is from the inside out. There is a way the glory of God will radiate in your life from inside if you fear God.

Also, as a woman, you have a lot of spiritual responsibilities to fulfill at home. Don't think virtuous women get married and relax in their husbands' houses without praying for their homes and husbands. This is why it is often said that there is a good woman behind every successful man, but I tell you the real thing is "that *there is a praying woman behind every successful man.* " If you are not serving God genuinely, you may be unable to fulfill this duty as a wife. Coming to God is the first step to having a beautiful home that will be the envy of many other women. It is said that a life without Christ is full of crisis, and so is also a home without Christ full of crisis.

Ecclesiastes 12:1-2 "Remember now thy
Creator in the days of thy youth, while the
evil days come not, nor the years draw nigh

when thou shalt say, I have no pleasure in them;

While the sun, or the light, or the moon, or the stars, be not darkened, nor the clouds return after the rain."

The best time to serve God and seek his face as a woman is now that you are young and single. Don't walk through life in confusion using your head knowledge because life is beyond that. Only your creator knows you better and knows the things that are best for you in life.

Proverbs 31:10

"Who can find a virtuous woman? For her price is far above rubies."

Every man desires a virtuous woman because she is to be treasured. The Bible says her price is far above rubies. You become desirable if you are virtuous, and you can't be a truly virtuous woman if you are not rooted in God and filled with the Holy Spirit. You have to decide to truly submit your life to Christ from this time so that he can fill you and guide your paths henceforth.

CHAPTER ELEVEN

PUTTING YOUR PERSONAL NEEDS ON MEN (ENTITLEMENT MENTALITY)

Let it not be that once a man proposes love to you, then the next thing you start presenting your bills to him. You must concentrate on building relationship with him first not how you will build your bank account from him. Most times billing in a relationship is a turn off for guys who.sinceressincererelationship with you.

Some ladies feel that their responsibilities and bills automatically become that man's duty once they meet any man who asks them out. This belief is called *entitlement mentality.*

I wonder how such ladies met their needs before coming across the man. I once met a beautiful lady, and we got talking. Barely two days after we met, she started telling me all her personal needs and bills that she had to pay. She also told me her mother had been sick and needed drugs, but there was no money for her to get the drugs. That day, I sent her some money to get medicines for her mother since her health is essential. Three days later, she told me her siblings needed money to attend school the following day. Her request usually comes with so much pressure as a matter of life or death. At this time, I was turned off and never called or took her calls anymore. She sent text messages to me pleading, but I never responded because, in the few days we spent together, I found out she believed I was responsible for all her family and personal bills.

I am not saying it's wrong for a guy to financially, emotionally, and otherwise support your needs, but you must know it is not your entitlement. Allow it to come from him naturally. You can share your needs with him, but he does not necessarily have to provide for you. Let it not be that once a man proposes love to you, then the next thing you start presenting your bills to him. You must concentrate on building a relationship with him first, not on how you will build your bank account from him. Usually, billing in a relationship is a turn-off for guys who want a sincere relationship with you.

Philippians 2:12

"Wherefore, my beloved, as ye have always obeyed, not as in my presence only, but now much more in my absence, work out your own salvation with fear and trembling."

The Bible talks about working out your salvation. It should be the same when it comes to your needs. You or your guardian should be able to meet your needs in whatever small way to avoid scaring suitors or friends from you. Any financial assistance or material thing that you can not request from your parents or guardian you should not request from someone who just came your way to have a genuine relationship with you. When a guy knows you and becomes more comfortable with you, he will meet your needs naturally without thinking twice because he knows you are not after what he can do for you. If you put your needs first, you cannot sustain any serious relationship. You will not be able to know the right man for you that way.

When I met my wife, she was still an undergraduate at the University. At that time, I knew she needed money to be able to meet a lot of demands in school. She was not on any scholarship or grant and was being trained in school by her mother, a widow. I often asked her if I could support her bills, but she always told me not to bother myself and that she would be good. It was quite some time before I could get her bank details and give her my support voluntarily. When I later asked her why she refused my offer to assist initially, she said she knew it was not my duty to train her in school but her parents' since we were not married. That statement made her earn respect for me, and I knew she was not after what she could get from me.

To earn respect as a lady, stop demanding and let it come at will. Anything received from someone with mounting pressure is not from a sincere heart. Giving is willingly. Some men would test you with money or gifts to know if you love them or are after what they offer. Unfortunately, not many ladies pass this test because they feel their responsibility is always to receive from men.

Meanwhile, in a relationship, giving should be reciprocal; you take and give. Don't always put yourself at the receiving end; it is called "*selfishness.*" If a man gifts you a phone, you should be able to buy him airtime. At times, when a man takes you out on a date, try to pay for the taxi if you can't pay for the meal. It shows that you are supportive and not in the relationship to exploit him.

I know a man who met with a particular lady, and they started a relationship. After some time, this lady started demanding all manner of things, and this man said he was doing it for her. Initially, he said he never had the plan to sleep with her since he wanted marriage and the fact that the lady was still a virgin, but when he discovered that the financial burdens and the demands from her were too much, he started asking her for sex until he eventually had his way. They later got separated, and the lady was crying. Most guys will start putting pressure on you to have you in their beds if your demands are too much on them because they are not sure if what you want is their money or the relationship, so they, too, want to have something in return.

2 Thessalonians 3:10

"For even when we were with you, this we commanded you, that if any would not work, neither should he eat."

You must have your source of income, no matter how little, to take care of your basic needs so that you can earn yourself some respect when you meet a man, and he will not be under pressure for any reason. Also, you need to be moderate and content in your demands and concentrate more on building relationships than being self-centered.

CHAPTER TWELVE

NOT TAKING CARE OF
YOUR BODY

---

*Taking care of your body as a lady may
include; caring for every health challenges
you have, taking your bath regularly,
smelling nice always, a good hair do,
wearing clean and fitting clothes, and
undies, keeping your environment clean.*

K eeping and maintaining a clean and healthy
lifestyle is a way of prolonging your life and
looking attractive to people. As a lady, one
of the things you must know is how to take care of your
body. I know many things can be a turn-off for men

when they meet a lady; one of them is when a lady cannot take care of herself.

Taking care of your body as a lady may include caring for every health challenge, bathing regularly, smelling nice always, a good hairdo, wearing clean and fitting clothes and undies, and keeping your environment clean.

3 John 1:2

"Beloved, I wish above all things that thou mayest prosper and be healthy, even as thy soul prospereth."

God wishes that we stay healthy even as our souls are healthy. Your look might be the first thing to invite a guy to you as a lady.

A woman is supposed to take her bath at least twice a day, both morning and night. Some ladies develop body odor and smell offensive due to not taking their baths regularly. Nobody is attracted to foul odor; it is a turn-off. Applying deodorants and body spray can go a long way to giving a lady a pleasant smell. Also, you must brush your teeth at least twice daily to keep your breath fresh. Always check and correct any odor from the mouth to avoid being offensive.

A good hair can also make a lady look attractive. If you are cutting your hair as a lady, you have to keep it short and clean always, and if you are making your hair, always make it at the right time. Leaving your hair dirty and tattered as a woman doesn't speak well of you. You must know the right hairstyles that fit you and stick to them always. In selecting your hair materials like attachments, you must know the right colors and keep them simple. Your hairstyle must not be the most expensive or flamboyant, but it just has to be simple and beautiful.

Additionally, your clothes should be clean, simple, and fitting to give you a sharp and attractive look. Your undies must be kept clean, too, to avoid infections due to dirt and germs. It is advisable to change your undies each time you have your bath.

Attention should also be given to your feet and nails. Keep your nails clean always and avoid dirt underneath.

If you are used to polishing your nails, don't allow it to go bad before changing the polish. Do pedicures, manicures, and facial treatments when necessary. Don't allow stripe marks on your foot, as they look unpleasant.

Find out a matching body cream and soap for your skin type. You don't necessarily have to bleach your skin to look good, but you have to maintain your natural skin color by keeping it glowing. Skin bleaching may later result in skin irritations and sometimes can lead to skin cancer.

Your room and the environment you stay in as a lady speaks volumes about you. Some ladies look good and beautiful outside, but you will be disappointed when you get to their rooms or environments. Clean and always make your environment look neat, like the usual saying, "*Charity begins at home.*"

If you have any health issue that requires medical attention, you don't need to postpone it. For instance, if you notice symptoms of an infection in your body, you must get treatment to avoid escalation. You must also have regular exercise and eat right always. Always remember that *staying healthy is staying wealthy.*

CHAPTER THIRTEEN

NOT BEING ABLE TO COOK AND DO HOUSEHOLD CHORES

Knowing how to cook as a lady is an additional value because it has been shown clearly that one of the ways to making a man happy is to prepare delicious meals for him.

The first day I ate a meal prepared by my wife was when I visited her in school with two of my colleagues from my office shortly before our wedding. For the first time, I felt like a great king in a royal palace as my wife was serving us. It was Nigerian jollof rice garnished with carrot, green beans, and other nutritious items, and it had a great, delicious taste. I could still remember how it tasted and how much of a mouth-watering experience we all had that night from the exquisite meal prepared by my wife.

Later on, I asked myself why it was difficult to forget that experience in a hurry; I had eaten in five-star restaurants and other beautiful cafés and tasted all manners of great meals prepared by hired intercontinental chefs. I then realized that it was not the taste of my wife's jollof rice alone that made it unforgettable but that it was prepared by someone dear to my heart.

Before I got married, I was an addicted restaurant lover, eating from one Cafe to another. When I finally married my wife, I did not need to eat at the restaurant because the meals she prepared at home most times beat the quality of what I ate outside. Also, I have more confidence in the process and composition of the food prepared by my wife at home. Additionally, I am not just eating the meal prepared by my wife but also have an emotional attachment to the fact that somebody I know is meeting a vital need that I had at that moment.

It's often said that "*the way to a man's heart is through his stomach*"; hence, one of the ways to win a man's heart is to prepare delicious meals for him.

Genesis 27:1-4

"And it came to pass, that when Isaac was old, and his eyes were dim so that he could not see, he called Esau his eldest son, and said unto him, My son: and he said unto him, Behold, here am I.

And he said, Behold now, I am old, I know not the day of my death:

Now therefore take, I pray thee, thy weapons, thy quiver, and thy bow, and go out to the field, and take me some venison;

And make me savory meat, such as I love, and bring it to me, that I may eat; that my soul may bless thee before I die."

At this time, what would provoke Isaac's blessings to his son was a delicious meal, and the hand of his son from whom the meal would come receives the blessing. As the popular Nigeria saying goes, *the way to a man's heart is through the stomach. Knowing* how to cook as a lady is an additional value because it has been shown clearly that one of the ways to make a man happy is to prepare delicious meals for him. However, in this generation, most people who can afford housemaids leave the burden of cooking and household chores for themselves. Some people hire chefs to prepare their meals, so the wife has no business with cooking. Well, having a housemaid or hired chef is good, maybe because of other engagements or to ease stress. But at the same time, a good woman should cook for her household occasionally. This is because there is an emotion attached to meeting the crucial needs of someone you love regularly, and one of them is food. Sometimes, we hear that some men sleep with their maids, and we often wonder why. It is because the maid meets their crucial needs, and they start basking in emotions with them over time.

This is not just in cooking alone but in other domestic chores. Let it be that you can prepare good meals and do house chores, but you are getting a housemaid to assist you while you do it by yourself once in a while.

The worst scenario is experienced when a family cannot afford a housemaid while the wife can't cook and is lazy about household chores. There will be a crisis in such homes.

I am not of the opinion that the man or the husband shouldn't do household chores or even cook, but the truth is that the wife has the primary responsibility for that. The husband also has that as his secondary responsibility. If you cannot cook as a single lady or are lazy about doing domestic chores, you will definitely not be able to do better as a married woman.

You must learn how to prepare various foods because you never can tell the one your family would love to have. The quality of your food determines how eager people would love to come around you to taste your meal. When I was growing up as a child, there were homes that we went to, and once meals were served, we didn't eat because we already knew over time that their food was not tasty, and if care is not taken when you eat their food, you can contract food poisoning. I remember eating a particular native soup (Okoho) of

Idoma land in one of my uncle's houses in the village when I was a little boy. I started throwing up immediately after the meal because the soup was poorly prepared, and since then, I have gotten irritated and stopped eating that native soup. At least let people know they are getting delicious meals from your hands anytime they visit, and you will see that your home will be welcoming to many visitors.

Doing household chores is also a form of exercise. It includes laundry, cleaning, dusting, grocery shopping, doing dishes, cleaning toilets, making beds, sweeping, feeding pets, etc. Those activities involve physical and mental exertions, making it a form of exercise. A special kind of joy is derived from keeping your home and environment always clean and sparkling.

As a lady, you must not make the mistake of not knowing how to cook or being lazy about household chores because this mistake will be a great minus for you. There are many platforms you can learn cooking from these days. If you are not privileged to learn cooking while growing up at home, you can enroll in one of the many available platforms. Also, start doing your household chores now until you master the act.

CHAPTER FOURTEEN

HAVING UNDEFINED AND WRONG RELATIONSHIPS

---

*Let all your relationship with the opposite
sex be spelt out and well defined. Know
those who are just casual friends, those who
are aliens and the one that is your intimate
friend.*

Being in the company of the opposite sex with
relationships undefined has a way of scaring
away the right relationship from you. You are
around Maxwell today. Tomorrow, you will be seen
with Josiah, and maybe the following day, you will be
with John. It doesn't speak well of you as a lady. You

may tell me you are benefiting from keeping many boyfriends, but you have to learn how to keep the boundaries and define the relationships where necessary. Otherwise, there may be a lot of drawbacks. Keeping more than one intimate boyfriend relationship at a time is an act of promiscuity.

Matthew 6:24

No man can serve two masters, for either he will hate and love the other, or he will hold to the one and despise the other. Ye cannot serve God and mammon.

The Bible passage above applies to God and mammon alone and is relevant to having more than one relationship. There is no way you can perfectly date more than one man simultaneously and be totally committed to both of them.

James 1:8: A double-minded man is unstable in all his ways.

While on campus at the university, I had no girl I could say I had a relationship with. I decided to practice relationships with girls during my compulsory National Youth Service year since I have not been doing that. I entered a relationship and later migrated from having one girlfriend to having four girlfriends simultaneously. At that time, those four girls were connected to me emotionally, and they all wanted to contact me simultaneously. I was responsible for giving all four of them my attention and care in return. I just did this for about two weeks and almost lost my breath because I couldn't meet their demands individually. The time, resources, attention, and care I shared with them were draining me out.

At last, I lost all of them because I had to give them total attention individually and not share it between them. Although among them, there was the one I loved most, she was the one I lost first because I was not entirely dedicated to her. I learned my lesson since then.

Some ladies also do this, thinking it is an act of smartness, or they may think they will understudy and choose the best out of the many. Relationships are not like that; we are not designed to serve two masters. I used to hear some ladies say, "Keeping all your eggs in one basket is dangerous." But in reality, keeping your eggs in one basket will make you concentrate and focus more on preserving them.

People watch you as you go out with different guys, but you may not know. People have their voices to lend when your matters are being discussed behind you, and they may create a negative impression about you. Remember, the truth is established in the mouth of two or more witnesses. I have come to understand that people's testimony about you also matters a lot, which is why keeping a clean slate is good.

Let all your relationships with the opposite sex be spelled out and well-defined. Know those who are just casual friends, those who are aliens, and those who are your intimate friends. Don't be putting your hands in bestie today; tomorrow is school father, and next is your paddy. Don't live a tattered life like that as a lady. You can make friends with men, but not everyone of them that you are seen around with always, and they are all calling and chatting with you. You are not a public service agent, so don't block your way unnecessarily by putting all manner of junk in your way.

Another mistake you may be making is surrounding yourself with the wrong female friends. The kind of female friends you keep around you can go a long way either to make you or mar you.

> *Psalms 1:1 Blessed is the man that walketh not in the counsel of the ungodly, nor standeth in the way of sinners, nor sitteth in the seat of the scornful.*

You can't walk together in bad company and say you are good. It is often said, "Show me your friend, and I will tell you who you are." People can easily interpret your character in your company because two cannot walk together unless they agree. If you follow girls who do wrong, you will start doing it one day. If your friends are smokers and drug addicts, you will follow suit in no time. Some wrong friends will betray you if care is not taken. I have seen several ladies introduce their friends to the men in their lives, only for the said friends to end up getting married to the men. This happens when a lady is not wise enough to select her friends carefully. Men are moved by what they see most of the time. The person you call your bestie might take advantage of you when there are cracks in your walls, mainly if the boundaries are not well kept. You have the access key to your life, so use it wisely.

It's only birds of the same feathers that flock together. You can never see eagles and chickens in the same company, nor the lion and the dog playing together in the field. Walking in the company of the wise can make you wise, and the company of fools can make you foolish.

If the friend you keep is always in competition with you, know she is jealous of you, and when she sees any good thing coming your way, she will destroy it. For instance, she wants to buy every new item of clothing or shoe you wear, by all means, not because she loves to be in uniform with you but maybe because she wants to compete with you and, if possible, become more than you. Such a friend will fight everything good coming to you. At times, you are with some friends who have made mistakes with their lives in the past, and instead of advising and watching your back so that you will not fall victim to similar mistakes, they will instead push you to do the same so that you will be equal. You must be wise enough to identify such people and never fall victim to their traps.

2 Corinthians 6:14

Be ye not unequally yoked together with unbelievers: for what fellowship hath righteousness with unrighteousness? and what communion hath light with darkness?

You cannot be unequally yoked with an unbeliever. Any human being who doesn't fear God is an endangered species; every evil thing is possible at any time with an unbeliever because God is not controlling the mind but by the devil. Morality is good but not good enough to keep someone from doing evil because a moral person who is not filled with the Holy Spirit is still subject to the dictate of the devil. You have the right to choose your friends. Friendship is not by force! Don't allow anybody to force themselves on you.

CHAPTER FIFTEEN

EXPOSING YOUR BODY (INDECENT DRESSING)

A virtuous woman dresses for strength of purpose and dignity not for slaying or killing. You don't dress to look hot but you dress to look royal.

All the most valuable things on earth are hidden. They can only be accessed by discovery. For instance, Gold is obtained from mining and crude oil is obtained from deep down the earth. On the contrary, all the cheap things in the world are commonly exposed and easily accessible. Anything that is too common cannot be expensive. The scarcity of a thing can always lead to inflation, and anything gotten with a high price is valuable.

While preparing for my wedding, I went to a wristwatch shop in Lagos, Nigeria. It was a very big jewelry shop with all kinds of jewelry. I started checking for the wristwatch right from the shop entrance. I noticed that the more I entered the shop, the higher the quality and prices of the wristwatches. I was still going until I got to the last row in the shop; there, I saw a unique showcase, and inside the showcase was the most expensive jewelry. Unlike other watches I saw in the shop before getting to those in the special showcase, you cannot touch watches in the showcase as they are under lock and key. I didn't need to ask why those watches were kept in the special showcase under lock and key because I knew that good and valuable things are not kept anyhow.

1 Timothy 2:9-10

"In like manner also, that women adorn themselves in modest apparel, with shamefacedness and sobriety; not with

broided hair, or gold, or pearls, or costly array;

But (which becometh women professing godliness) with good works. "

The way a woman dresses determines her value and her rating. How people rate you determines how you will be addressed. It is not every woman that all men can stop on the road anyhow. When men see a harlot on the road, they know; when they see a wife material, they learn from the look. So many men go after women who expose their bodies because they know they are easily accessible and are in active public service. But if they see a well-dressed decent lady, they adjust their minds before going to such a lady because they are going there for something serious. Men know the girls they can mess up with and the girls whose dignity is intact. The impression most African men have is that if you are not adequately dressed or choose to dress indecently, it means you have nothing else to offer but your body.

If you are wondering why your relationship doesn't last, you may have to check your dress because the first impression you create in people's minds by your dress makes them want to come and eat and go. They didn't mean to come and stay because your pose shows that you are public property. Any man you attract by being naked will leave you when he sees another lady who is more naked than you.

Any dress that is suggestive, revealing, and seductive is wrong. You don't need to expose sensitive parts of your body. People will be after your body; they may not necessarily want you for a wife. Give yourself some respect by dressing to cover your nakedness.

Proverbs 11:22

"As a jewel of gold in a swine's snout, so is a fair woman without discretion."

Beauty is not in being naked or dressing indecently, but true beauty is in covering yourself. The Bible says if you show no discretion as a woman, you are like a gold ring in a pig's snout. If you put a golden ring on a pig's nose, it will look very dirty very soon.

Following fashion trends blindly is not what is expected of a virtuous woman. You must not put on all the categories of chains and rings available. Beauty is not all about piercing every part of your body to put rings or tattoo your body all in the name of fashion. Before you go after any fashion style, you must try to find out about the origin and why people dress that way.

Proverbs 31:25

"Strength and honor are her clothing; and she shall rejoice in time to come."

A virtuous woman dresses for strength of purpose and dignity, not for slaying or killing. You don't dress to look hot, but you dress to look royal. Some ladies model their lives after the pattern of the world, not God's kingdom. You are of royal blood, and you are not cheap but expensive. You cannot see anybody from the royal family dress anyhow because there is a pattern of dress that befits them. No wonder the royal family commands much respect because nothing makes them compromise their dressing standard. Anywhere you see royalty, you will know, and you don't need anybody to tell you before you address them that way.

Do a personal assessment of yourself any time you dress; ask yourself the motive behind that dress pattern. Is it to glorify God or to draw the wrong people to you? Remember, the way you dress is the way you will be addressed.

CHAPTER SIXTEEN

ABORTION AND BIRTH CONTROL PILLS

According to the design of God, any child that is conceived deserves the right to live and be given birth to. Unfortunately, some ladies are fond of doing this gruesome cruelty without considering the repercussions. There are many repercussions to commiting abortion.

It is very offensive for an older woman to cough into a pot of soup, and as if that is not enough, she starts using her underwear to clean that pot. Automatically, she is guilty of two offenses; firstly, coughing into the pot of soup is a great offense. Secondly, using her underwear to clean the pot is a greater offense. Getting pregnant as a single lady is sinful, but going to the extent of committing an abortion is an abomination. If you are guilty of one, you don't have to be guilty of the other.

Nowadays, abortion has become very rampant among single ladies. In many nations of the world, this act has become legalized. Meanwhile, some countries that know the negative impact of this inhuman act have refused to participate.

Abortion means killing a fetus while still in the womb. It is not an act of removing clotted blood from the womb but an intentional process of using medicine, techniques, or tools to terminate the life of an unborn child. According to the design of God, any child that is conceived deserves the right to live and be given birth to. Unfortunately, some ladies are fond of doing this gruesome cruelty without considering the repercussions. There are many repercussions to committing abortion.

Firstly, abortion is an act of murder. Some people feel that it is a fetus, so it doesn't amount to killing since the child has not yet given birth. There are no two words for it other than the murder of an innocent child who, if given the opportunity, will live and fulfill their purpose as a human being.

Exodus 23:7

Keep thee far from a false matter; and the innocent and righteous slay thou not: for I will not justify the wicked.

Leviticus 24:17

And he that killeth any man shall surely be put to death.

God uses strong words when it comes to taking another person's life. This is because no human being has the power to create another human being or give life. The lives of men, young or old, are precious to God, so anybody who takes another person's life invites God's judgment. Before a child is formed in her mother's womb, God has already designed the destiny of such a child and the purpose to be fulfilled. So, any child terminated in the womb is like tampering with the order of God on earth. Getting pregnant is beyond just a normal biological process; if not, how do you explain situations where couples medically proven to be okay and all biological requirements met cannot conceive?

Genesis 4:8-12

And Cain talked with Abel, his brother: and it came to pass, when they were in the field, that Cain rose up against Abel, his brother, and slew him.

And the LORD said unto Cain, Where is Abel thy brother? And he said, I know not: Am I my brother's keeper?

And he said, What hast thou done? The voice of thy brother's blood crieth unto me from the ground.

And now art thou cursed from the earth, which hath opened her mouth to receive thy brother's blood from thy hand;

When thou tillest the ground, it shall not henceforth yield unto thee her strength; a fugitive and a vagabond shalt thou be in the earth.

The first case of killing that was recorded on earth was when Cain killed his brother Abel. The blood of Abel cried from the world to God in heaven, and it instigated God's judgment instantly. Any blood spilled on earth has a voice, and it reaches out to the heavens, as its consequence is a curse directly from God.

In every law court on earth, the act of murder is a punishable offense. Usually, the penalty is a death sentence or life imprisonment. This is to say that anyone who kills is also worthy of death. God is merciful, but if he didn't pass judgment immediately, it doesn't mean that he will not pass judgment again. If you have been involved in this act, you must confess it and seek God's mercy and forgiveness. Whether you did it yourself or helped someone do it, you need the mercy of God.

Secondly, apart from God's judgment on abortions, there are numerous health consequences of this act. It can lead to damage to the womb or cervix, putting the woman at risk of not conceiving and bearing children in the future. It may also result in infection of the uterus or the fallopian tube. Abortion may weaken the cervix, which increases a woman's risk of future pre-term deliveries.

Thirdly, in the worst cases where there are complications, abortion may result in death. According to the World Health Organization (WHO), about 68,000 women die every year from unsafe abortions, making it one of the leading causes of maternal mortality (13%). This means that every eight minutes, a woman in a developing nation will die of complications arising from unsafe abortion.

Don't make the mistake that will keep you in regret for the rest of your life. You may be running from one prayer house to another if you do. Also, don't do what will bring a generational curse upon your children.

If you get pregnant, it is better to give birth than staining your hands with blood. The shame and reproach are temporal, and you can get back to God again and make this right. It is better to bear the shame and reproach of men than guilt and judgment over your life. Giving birth outside wedlock might not be a hindrance to you getting married or achieving the plans of God for you in life if you genuinely repent and turn to God. Who knows if that baby will be your helper later in life? Moreover, it is crucial to stay away from premarital sex to avoid so many troubles that might follow consequently.

Taking Birth Control Pills by single ladies is also a thing of serious concern nowadays. This negatively affects the body of users, either short-term or long-term. Findings show that this can result in Cardiovascular problems such as heart attack, stroke, and blood clots. It may also result in cancers such as Breast Cancer and Cervical Cancer. It may alter your menstrual cycles.

The Biblical standard and prescription for living a sane life and not getting involved in things that will bring complications in your life is to stay away from sexual immorality. Sexual immorality is a sin! No wonder the scripture calls it "*a sin against your own body,*" maybe because of the likely consequences that are directed against your health.

CHAPTER SEVENTEEN

NOT HAVING VALUES
TO OFFER

---

*The amount of value you bring to the table
as a woman determines the respect you get
from your man. Certificates are good but
you must have something you can do
practically with your hands along with it.*

A woman of honor is a woman who is up and doing, not a woman who is a liability waiting for who will marry her and start bearing all her responsibilities without any contribution from her. Women are powerful, but it becomes evident only when they put their potential in them into creating value.

Proverbs 31:10-15

Who can find a virtuous woman? For her price is far above rubies.

The heart of her husband doth safely trust in her so that he shall have no need of spoil.

She will do him good and not evil all the days of her life.

She seeketh wool and flax and worketh willingly with her hands.

She is like the merchants' ships; she bringeth her food from afar.

She riseth also while it is yet night and giveth meat to her household and a portion to her maidens.

Things are changing, so the belief that women are to bear children and take care of household chores is no longer in vogue. The economy and society demand that women, too, should have something to bring to the table to support their husbands in some areas, no matter how little. This doesn't mean that women are primarily responsible for providing for the home, but they must be a support system.

It is good that you learn something and know how to at least do something with your hands, especially as a single lady. Although we hope for the best in marriage, we must also remember that sometimes the tides can also be against the ship in marriage. When all the chips are down, you are expected to be a backup for your household.

Many things can happen in marriage, and all those things are expected in one stage of the marriage or the other. Different marriages experience different situations. A man may lose his job or resign from his job while expecting another job, but it may not come immediately as expected; if there is no backup, then the family will suffer. Also, a man who is into business may face challenges sometimes, and the business may not bring anything to the table at that time, so a bit of support from the wife will go a long way. There are also situations where the woman may lose her husband,

and the children will start suffering because she has nothing to do that can bring food to the table.

You must learn a trade: fashion, makeup, hairdressing, graphics, baking, or any legitimate thing that can bring money. You can also be involved in any act of service that can be a source of income. Just learn whatever genuine things you can put together to turn into money.

Men derive special joy in knowing that their wives are resourceful. This also makes it easier for a young man to walk up to you as a single lady with something doing with her hands than one who is idle from morning till night and only on social media, wasting helpful time. Some ladies will say, "But I am still in school. That is why I have not learned any skill or trade", but school is not an excuse. You can be in school and squeeze out little time to acquire a skill if you prioritize it. The earlier, the better to get something done with your hands. I have seen some ladies who foot their bills in school from the handiwork they do even while they are still in school, and it didn't affect their academics in any way. You will become much more respected and less dependent when you have something to do with your hands.

The amount of value you bring to the table as a woman determines the respect you get from your man. Certificates are good, but you must have something you can do practically with your hands. Having the certificate and something you can create with your hands will be an advantage. This will keep you busy, and life will not be boring. Not all men may want their wives to do corporate-paid jobs, but if you have creative work, you can even do that from the comfort of your home or environment.

Be determined to be creative today and have value to offer any man that comes your way. Men are dazed when they meet you doing something. They know that you are resourceful and not a total liability. It is not only makeup that can bring the beauty of a woman out, but what she can create with her hands makes her even more beautiful.

CHAPTER EIGHTEEN

EXCESSIVE LOVER OF FUN

Depending on fun alone is like you want to take your car on a long journey and the only thing you check is whether the horn is working well. There are other vital and basic things which are even more important than the horn. Much more than enjoyment and pleasure are other things of life.

I once met a lady, and all she knew and kept talking about was the kinds of foods and drinks, all the best restaurants in town, and the best clubhouses and recreational centers. All she boasts about is how she has eaten in an expensive place and would love to go to the next place in town to have fun. Nothing more but fun!

I am not against having fun or going to places for relaxation or holidays, but it isn't good if it is too much. Every human should go out at least once in a while to see and feel a new environment as it improves physical and psychological health, but when it becomes all your essence in life, you are getting it wrong.

1 Corinthians 10:31

Whether you eat, drink, or whatever ye do,
do all to the glory of God.

As you go about having fun, let it be to the glory of God. Most importantly, life doesn't consist of food and drinks alone. All those things are good but should not be the primary thing life depends on. Depending on fun alone is like you want to take your car on a long journey, and the only thing you check is whether the horn is working well. Other vital things are even more critical than the horn. Much more than enjoyment and pleasure are other things in life.

Living a fun-filled life can be expensive. To have fun is not cheap; either you are paying for it or another person is paying. The money some ladies have used to have fun is enough to buy a plot of land somewhere or to invest in some profitable business. Some waste useful time that could have been used for other essential things of tangible value to catch unnecessary fun. If you meet a man and all you demand is how to have the best of fun with his hard-earned money, he may not take you seriously. Learn how to be moderate in all your doings.

Stop looking for all the five-star restaurants in town and who will take you there because that is not all that life entails. Some people will always say that the essence of life is to live and enjoy and that, after all, you will not go with anything from this world except what you have enjoyed. As pleasant and encouraging as this statement sounds, it is wrong because enjoyment itself is vanity, and you cannot take it anywhere when you die.

We all have different perceptions of the word enjoyment. At times, your enjoyment might be an allergy for me. For instance, you may call eating jollof rice and chicken enjoyable, but it is possible that any time I eat, it might distort my body system. Maybe you like going out to the beach to have a good view and swim in the water, and doing that might be more pleasurable to you than anything else, but I have seen people who said they don't go to the beach because they don't like swimming and the look of the water scares them. This clearly shows that the idea of enjoyment can not be generalized, and by so doing, it is considered vanity. Whatsoever on earth that cannot last forever and does not apply to every human is considered vanity.

Ecclesiastes 11:9-10

Rejoice, O young man, in thy youth; and let
thy heart cheer thee in the days of thy
youth, and walk in the ways of thine heart,
and in the sight of thine eyes: but know
thou, that for all these things God will bring
thee into judgment.

Therefore remove sorrow from thy heart,
and put away evil from thy flesh: for
childhood and youth are vanity.

You will realize that the Bible says you should enjoy yourself, but in the end, you will give an account of everything. Solomon followed his heart to get everything he wanted; at least he tasted everything he desired, but he later regretted it and said everything was vanity, including having fun. According to the wisest king that has ever lived on earth, everything in life concludes that "*man should fear God and keep his commandments as everything else a man does is vanity.*"

This same fad to have fun makes some ladies go from one clubhouse to another. You must know the limit of where you can go, all in the name of having fun as a child of God. You must not crave everywhere or everything just because you want to have fun. If you have no control over your fun life, it becomes excessive and a sin.

CHAPTER NINETEEN

SMOKING, DRINKING, AND SUBSTANCE ABUSE

Your body doesn't belong to you but it belongs to God, it is the temple of God. How can you destroy temple by your own hands? This is why you don't need to argue whether smoking, drinking or other substances abuse are sin or not.

Smoking, drinking, and substance abuse can be addictive, and it starts gradually. It is the height of irresponsibility to be drinking or smoking as a lady, knowing so many consequences that may result.

Taking alcohol can cause liver and heart diseases in women. It can also result in cancer. Women who drink are much more prone to sexual violence and abuse than those who don't drink and get drunk. It is very easy to get raped when you are drunk as a lady, as we have seen such cases happen.

Ladies who smoke encounter some issues shortly or later on in their lives. Smoking may affect the unborn child and result in low birth weight and other complications. Other health issues that may result from smoking include respiratory diseases like Chronic Obstructive Pulmonary Disease (COPD). This disease makes it difficult to breathe, and it gets worse over time. Also, Cardiovascular (heart) disease may be one of the effects of smoking in women. Research shows that women who smoke have a greater risk of dying quickly from heart-related diseases than their peers who don't smoke.

Additionally, people who smoke have an increased risk of many cancers, such as lung, pancreatic, kidney, liver, throat, bladder, and colorectal cancers. Cervical

Cancer is also associated with smoking. Smoking can also lead to depression and other mental illnesses. Some lunatics you see on the street are a result of marijuana and substance abuse.

Other substance abuse is highly detrimental to health. Some women use these substances to get high and have some sense of momentary pleasure. Substances abused may include prescription and over-the-counter medicine, heroin, cocaine, marijuana, ice, shisha, etc. Those substances taken outside prescriptions are very harmful to the health. You must desist from every temptation to harm yourself by your own hands.

1 Corinthians 3:16-17

Know ye not that ye are the temple of God,
and that the Spirit of God dwelleth in you?

If any man defile the temple of God, him
shall God destroy; for the temple of God is
holy, which temple ye are.

Your body doesn't belong to you, but it belongs to God; it is the temple of God. How can you destroy God's temple with your own hands? This is why you don't need to argue whether smoking, drinking, or other substance abuse are sins or not. It simply means destroying your body, which is God's temple, and God said anyone who destroys his temple shall be destroyed, too.

If you are involved in any of those things, you are making a great mistake and must quit immediately before it is too late. You must ask God for mercy and the grace to never return to it again. You may also visit a counselor for help where necessary. It's better to save your future now as a single lady.

CHAPTER TWENTY

BEING DECEIVED IN A RELATIONSHIP

You must take time to pray, watch and understudy any man that is coming your way. Don't be quick to throw yourself in any man's bed and started regretting later when he leaves you.

Many ladies rush into a relationship and quickly rush out because they didn't get it right from the beginning. The fact is that ninety percent of men who say "I love you" don't mean it so. They may be after you for sex, or they may be after what you have as a lady. Sometimes, they want to get closer to you to finally decide whether to take you seriously.

Matthew 10:16-17

Behold, I send you forth as sheep in the midst of wolves: be ye therefore wise as serpents and harmless as doves.

But beware of men: for they will deliver you up to the councils, and they will scourge you in their synagogues;

Ladies, you have to be wise and know what you are doing. If not, you will suffer much heartbreak, and some men will defraud you of your possessions or use you to get the opportunity for a better life. Only the wisdom of God can guide you through this, and it is the more reason you should have a close relationship with God so that he can direct you in all your ways.

While I was at the University those days, a neighbor had already graduated and was doing his National Youth Service. He had a girlfriend who used to come every weekend to cook, clean, and wash for him. This girl used all her life to serve the guy; sometimes, she would use her money to buy stuff and cook for my neighbor, buy gifts, and take him out occasionally. Somehow, we all knew that my neighbor was not ready to settle down with this lady, but she didn't realize it herself because her mind was beclouded by love and affection or probably out of desperation. Shortly a year later, after the guy finished his National Youth Service, he married another lady.

You will miss it if you appear too desperate to have any man come your way. You don't have to put yourself under any unnecessary pressure for any man. If not, you will end up shooting yourself in the leg. You must pray, watch, and understudy any man coming your way. Don't be quick to throw yourself in any man's bed and start regretting it later when he leaves you. We have said before that men who want something serious with you will not rush you for sex, and they will not leave you because you refused to have sex with them. We are emphasizing this because when a man sleeps with you as a woman, you become too emotionally attached to him. At that time, you will become blind to the fundamental things you must check out for in a relationship.

A man can give you anything or do anything for you to get you back on his bed, and you may think he is doing all those things for you because he loves you. Doing something for you or buying you things is not an assurance that a man loves you. Although when a man loves you, he does things for you, that is not enough evidence that a man loves you.

Proverbs 18:16: A man's gift makes room for him and brings him before great men.

Some men give you gifts to have access to you, and it doesn't matter the cost; they don't mind sacrificing it to get you and go after they have gotten what they want, then you will be wondering if it is not the same guy that brought you expensive phone or car. Every young lady needs the wisdom and the spirit of discernment from God.

You often find it difficult to know the man who loves you because of your selfish desires—assuming two people come to ask for your hand in marriage simultaneously. One has a broad chest and seemingly looks rich from a wealthy background. The second person is not wealthy-looking and not as handsome as the picture you always have. You may want to go for the first guy because you already have that standard in mind, although you are not sure if he loves you. You didn't even pray about it nor give a second thought because you saw a big car and a flashy, handsome-looking man. When he later uses you and dumps you, you will be heartbroken.

Meanwhile, the second guy may not have it all, but he will respect and love you. He will listen to you and work together with you to become the man you dreamed of having. The fact that a man is handsome or huge does not suggest that he would be a good husband, a loving father, and a responsible man. It is often not because God doesn't answer our prayers or give us what we desire, but he usually shows us raw materials to work on to become what we want.

Another thing that can help you know whether you are with the right person in a relationship is to get a mature and God-fearing counselor who is well-versed in the issues of relationships to advise you. Some people with the spirit of God are seasoned in understanding that you can share relationship issues with them, and they will guide you. This is why you must not keep your relationship to yourself alone, but you must have somebody to whom you can give an account for proper counseling. If not, you would have made an irredeemable mistake before you realized it.

Additionally, you must bring your partner to accountability at some point in your relationship. Make him know that you have somebody or people you report to, either your pastor, counselor, or parents/guardians. Men have a way of being cautious when you introduce them to a senior person in your life. They will be aware that it is not you and them alone, so they will not try to mess you up and go. Also, try to know the important senior person in their lives and ensure you are introduced to them. Don't just depend on the fact that you know their friends alone, their friends cannot call them to order most times when they are wrong. At times, most of the things guys do with you in a relationship are planned and discussed with their friends.

When you begin to see some red flags, don't ignore them. For instance, he started beating you up, threatens to hit you, goes out with another woman, abuses you verbally, lies to you often, doesn't not trust you, drinks and smokes, has no interest in the things of God, has uncontrollable anger, only loves you when you do or give him things, and not showing much concern about things that pertain to your future or personal progress. You need to watch out if you find those signs and confront him politely, but he doesn't change. It is possible he doesn't love you, or that is his character, and he doesn't just want to change. Whatever a man does to you while you are still single, he will do worse when you finally get married.

You have no reason to waste your time with someone who doesn't love you or value you because your waiting can't change anything. The power to change a human being is not in our hands but in the hands of the Holy Spirit. The right person will come your way if you stay positive.

CHAPTER TWENTY ONE

LIVING WITH YOUR PAST

Holding onto your past makes it your present life and it will keep hurting you as if it is just happening now. Were you raped as a child, abused, dumped by the person you love so much, impregnated, had an abortion, drugged, bullied, traumatized, or whatsoever be your experience? You have just got to let go if not it will keep on hurting you forever.

E very human being has a past, present, and future. The one you left behind is your past, the one you hold onto is your present, and the one you hold onto today determines your future.

Holding onto your past makes it your present life, and it will keep hurting you as if it is just happening now.

Were you raped as a child, abused, dumped by the person you love so much, impregnated, had an abortion, drugged, bullied, traumatized, or whatsoever be your experience? You have just got to let go. If not, it will keep on hurting you forever.

When you forgive the person who hurt you, you have not only let go of your past but also restored your peace of mind. If you see a lady holding onto some hurts in her mind, you will know because it tells everything she does.

Moving on in life means letting go and forgetting what is behind you. If my hands are clinched to the signage poles on my street, I am not going anywhere till Jesus comes as long as I hold on to them unless I let go. It is very unwise to keep myself in such bondage.

2 Corinthians 5:17

Therefore, if any man is in Christ, he is a
new creature: old things are passed away;
behold, all things have become new.

If you are in Christ, you become a new you. Therefore, the old you passed away. This understanding has a way of helping you tremendously as a lady. Clear your head and clean some junk in your mind because they are like a virus in your system. One thing is possible in life: moving on and starting with a new page, but you must first close the old pages of your life.

I know a lady who was said to be raped at a tender age. She kept those pictures in her mind for years, and all other men who came her way were irritating her until she opened up to a counselor. She was able to let go, and that was when she was set free from that mental bondage.

Anything that you can't change, you don't need to bother yourself and lock yourself in that prison. Worry doesn't change anything! Talk to somebody you trust about your past and the hurts you feel, and in that way, you feel relieved and let it go. A problem shared with the right person is a problem solved. You may have learned some lessons from that to help you make better decisions next time, but you must not allow that to torment you.

There is nothing you are passing through today that is peculiar to you alone or that nobody has experienced before and overcome.

A story was told of a man who lost his pair of shoes. He went about from door to door in his neighborhood, looking for his missing shoes because they were his favorite shoes that got missing. He eventually got to a door, and when he knocked, the door was opened. Behold, the man who opened the door was in a wheelchair with both his legs amputated. Reluctantly, he told the man in the wheelchair that he was looking for his missing favorite shoes. The man in the wheelchair said that if shoes were his problem, he could have quickly gone to buy a new pair, but his problem is getting a new pair of legs. The man looking for his missing shoes learned a lesson instantly and started weeping. Beyond what you think is your problem is another person's bigger problem.

A woman I respect so much is Joyce Meyer. She was a victim of sexual abuse by her own father right from when she was very young. She was raped by her father more than two hundred times. It didn't stop until she eventually left home when she was eighteen, spoke up, and got help. She is the president of Joyce Meyer Ministries, a charismatic Christian author and speaker worldwide.

Many health issues can be traced to what people keep in their minds. Living with hurt and bitterness can cause physical stress on your body, affect your central nervous system (CNS), and cause Cardiovascular issues like high blood pressure and heart disease. It also affects your excretory and digestive systems, and it can trigger your flight-or-fight stress response and release a flood of chemicals and hormones, like adrenaline, into your system, causing your immune system disorder.

You can never become what God wants you to be or fulfill your purpose in life if you live with hurt and bitterness in your mind. Consciously come out of your past experiences or present secrets that hurt you and let God work on your mind so that you can fulfill your destiny in life. You have to constantly renew and replace your mind of every pain with the word of God and the power of the Holy Spirit. There is no past that you can't conquer, and until you can conquer your past before, you can become what God destined you to be.

A WORD OF ENCOURAGEMENT

The Bible, in Proverbs 31, defines a virtuous woman as one who leads her home with respect, discipline, integrity, and more. All the virtues she practices aim to improve her husband's life, teach her children, and serve God. This, essentially, is the meaning of a virtuous woman.

God designed every lady to be a virtuous woman. Every man's dream is to have one; even society holds the place of a virtuous woman in high esteem.

This can be possible if you follow this book's steps and avoid mistakes that can mar your life as a lady. Also, you will have a beautiful family where you don't have to live in regrets, enjoy a healthy life, and reach a desirable societal place.

It doesn't matter if you have gotten some things wrong in your life already. Pick up your life again and start on a fresh note; shortly, you will be amazed at how God will fix you up.

I sincerely pray for you and trust God that his desires for your life will be fulfilled, and someday, I will hear your testimony in Jesus' name. Amen.